YOUR KNOWLEDGE HAS VALUE

- We will publish your bachelor's and
  master's thesis, essays and papers

- Your own eBook and book -
  sold worldwide in all relevant shops

- Earn money with each sale

Upload your text at www.GRIN.com
and publish for free

Philipp Schweers

The 'Democratic Peace' proposition and democracies using military force

GRIN Verlag

Bibliografische Information der Deutschen Nationalbibliothek:

Die Deutsche Bibliothek verzeichnet diese Publikation in der Deutschen National-
bibliografie; detaillierte bibliografische Daten sind im Internet über http://dnb.d-
nb.de/ abrufbar.

Dieses Werk sowie alle darin enthaltenen einzelnen Beiträge und Abbildungen
sind urheberrechtlich geschützt. Jede Verwertung, die nicht ausdrücklich vom
Urheberrechtsschutz zugelassen ist, bedarf der vorherigen Zustimmung des Verla-
ges. Das gilt insbesondere für Vervielfältigungen, Bearbeitungen, Übersetzungen,
Mikroverfilmungen, Auswertungen durch Datenbanken und für die Einspeicherung
und Verarbeitung in elektronische Systeme. Alle Rechte, auch die des auszugsweisen
Nachdrucks, der fotomechanischen Wiedergabe (einschließlich Mikrokopie) sowie
der Auswertung durch Datenbanken oder ähnliche Einrichtungen, vorbehalten.

Imprint:

Copyright © 2009 GRIN Verlag GmbH
Druck und Bindung: Books on Demand GmbH, Norderstedt Germany
ISBN: 978-3-656-41533-6

This book at GRIN:

http://www.grin.com/en/e-book/129263/the-democratic-peace-proposition-and-
democracies-using-military-force

GRIN - Your knowledge has value

Der GRIN Verlag publiziert seit 1998 wissenschaftliche Arbeiten von Studenten, Hochschullehrern und anderen Akademikern als eBook und gedrucktes Buch. Die Verlagswebsite www.grin.com ist die ideale Plattform zur Veröffentlichung von Hausarbeiten, Abschlussarbeiten, wissenschaftlichen Aufsätzen, Dissertationen und Fachbüchern.

Visit us on the internet:

http://www.grin.com/

http://www.facebook.com/grincom

http://www.twitter.com/grin_com

Philipp Schweers

LL.M. Law & Politics of International Security
Assignment International Security

The "Democratic Peace" proposition and democracies using military force

"As culture grows and men gradually move towards greater agreement over their principles, they lead to mutual understanding and peace."[1]

The theory of democratic peace is perhaps one of the most widely accepted propositions among international relations scholars today. A vast body of literature, from theoretical elaborations to statistical measurements, concerning liberal peace and/or democratic peace theory[2] has been developed and has explored the proposition profoundly.[3]

The theoretical background dates back to Immanuel Kant's writings in the 18th century, especially to the ideas in his "Perpetual Peace" treatise,[4] but with the late 1980s – the end of the Cold War – an explosion of scholarly interest in the topic of democratic peace has taken place. Although there exists a dissenting minority[5], the consensus among the great majority of scholars claims that democratic states/liberal democracies do not or are "less likely to fight wars with each other".[6]

"[The] absence of war between democratic states comes as close as anything we have to an empirical law in international relations."[7]

Recently, this opinion or discussion enhanced its scope. It left the dimension of academia while reaching the policy-level of Western countries, namely the U.S..[8]

---

[1] Immanuel Kant, 'Kant's Political Writings', Hans Reiss (ed.), H.B. Nisbet (trans.), Cambridge: Cambridge University Press, 1970, p. 114.

[2] Michael Doyle in his pioneering work, 'Kant, Liberal Legacies, and Foreign Affairs', *Philosophy and Public Affairs*, Vol. 12, No. 3 (Summer, 1983), pp. 205-235, applied the theory to what he called "Liberal states" which he defined as "States with some form of representative democracy, a market economy based on private property rights, and constitutional protections of civil and political rights" (207-208). The theory is sometimes called the "Liberal peace theory". Within this paper, I use the terms "Liberal peace theory" and "Democratic peace theory" synonymously.

[3] For an excellent overview of the current 'state of the art', see James Lee Ray, 'Does Democracy Cause Peace?', *Annual Review of Political Science*, 1 (1998), pp. 27–46.

[4] Immanuel Kant, 'Perpetual Peace' (1795) in The Philosophy of Kant, ed. Carl J. Friedrich, New York: Modem Library, 1949

[5] See e.g. Christopher Layne, 'Kant or Cant: The Myth of the Democratic Peace', *International Security*, 19:2 (Fall 1994), pp. 5–49; David E. Spiro, 'The Insignificance of the Liberal Peace', *International Security*, 19:2 (Fall 1994), pp. 50-86.

[6] David A. Lake, 'Powerful Pacifists: Democratic States and War', *American Political Science Review*, 86:1 (March 1992), p. 32. Democratic peace proponents often claim that democracies do not wage war against each other. Some scholars, inter alia David A. Lake, modified the thesis toward 'less likely'.

[7] Jack S. Levy, 'The Causes of War: A Review of Theories and Evidence', in Philip E. Tetlock/Jo L. Husbands/Robert Jervis/Paul C. Stern/Charles Tilly (eds.), 'Behavior, Society, and Nuclear War', Vol. 1, New York: Oxford University Press, 1989, p. 270.

But, although wars between democracies are seemingly absent, this does not mean that liberal states are totally reluctant to use military force or to fight wars. Concerning this it is to say that the idea of democratic peace does not only include the thesis that wars between democracies are less/not likely to appear.

Since the substantial scientific discussion concerning democratic peace has accelerated in the late 1980s/early 1990s, four other characteristics of the democratic peace have been formulated.

First, proponents of the democratic peace argue that democracies tend to win through wars they fight with nondemocracies.[9] Second, some scholars pointed out that democracies suffer less casualties and fight shorter in wars that are initialized by them, compared with non-democratic states.[10] Third, it has been underlined that liberal democracies which face serious disputes with democratic peers opt for more peaceful or mitigating means of conflict resolution than other (non-democratic) dyads in conflict.[11] Fourth and finally, scholars like Randall Schweller brought forward the argument that powerful democracies do not engage in preventive wars.[12]

While it is almost empirically proven that the probability of wars between democratic states is very low or even zero,[13] war is obviously – while having a look on recent or current

---

[8] See e.g. Condoleeza Rice (former secretary of state),'The Promise of Democratic Peace', Washington Post December 11, 2005, accessed at: http://www.washingtonpost.com/wp-dyn/content/article/2005/12/09/AR2005120901711.html (visited January 22, 2009)

[9] Concerning this argumentation, see e.g. David A. Lake, 'Powerful Pacifists: Democratic States and War', *supra* note 6.

[10] See Randolph M. Siverson, 'Democracies and War Participation: In Defense of the Institutional Constraints Argument', *European Journal of International Relations*, 1 (December 1995), pp. 481–490.

[11] Compare e.g. Michael Mousseau, 'Democracy and Compromise in Militarized Interstate Conflicts, 1816–1992', *Journal of Conflict Resolution*, 42:2 (April 1998), pp. 210–230; William J. Dixon, 'Democracy and the Peaceful Settlement of International Conflict', *American Political Science Review*, 88:1 (March 1994), pp. 14–32.

[12] Randall Schweller, 'Domestic Structure and Preventive War: Are Democracies More Pacific?', *World Politics*, 44:2 (January 1992), pp. 235–269. With the emerge of the Bush Doctrine of "acting against emerging threats before they are fully formed" within the National Security Strategy of the United States of 2002 and with the American intervention in Iraq, this claim of democratic peace is obviously falsified. See Duncan E. J. Currie, '"Preventive War" and International Law after Iraq', accessed at: http://www.globelaw.com/Iraq/Preventive_war_after_iraq.htm (visited January 22, 2009).

[13] Zeev Maoz/Bruce M. Russett, 'Normative and Structural Causes of Democratic Peace, 1946–1986', *American Political Science Review*, 87:3 (September 1993), pp. 624–638.

armed conflicts in which democratic states are engaged – still an option for liberal democracies with regards to disputes with non-democratic states.

On a first glance this seems to be paradox. But while having a deeper look into the scientific discussions, approaches and explanations, it seemingly becomes clear that these two parts – namely the peaceful conflict-resolution between democratic states and democracies' use of military force – are not conflicting.

Generally speaking, three major basic approaches for the explanation of the existence of democratic peace exist and each one describes different mechanisms and drivers toward the absence of war among democracies:

1. The institutionalist approach, based on rationalism and explaining the absence of war among democracies through the existence of democratic institutions which place constraints to the democratic leaders

2. The constructivist approach, explaining the absence of war through shared norms and values of democratic societies.

3. The interdependence approach, explaining that increasing economic interconnection between states reduces the risk of war.

Within the next paragraphs I will briefly examine the different approaches of explanation of the democratic peace and will underscore their inherent mechanisms used to explain it. Furthermore, I will analyze to what extent the explanations for the democratic peace within these approaches may also account for the use of military force by liberal democracies.

The rationalist explanation/The institutional approach

One popular approach in explaining democratic peace is based on instititutional arguments. Within this way of explaining liberal peace, democratic institutions are seen to be the fundamental cause of peace among democracies.

First, it is argued that the legal and constitutional system of restraints on executive action which exists in democratic states, the system of 'checks and balances', are narrowing the scope for adversial actions against others and therefore protect peace for several reasons.[14]

Second, in combination with domestic democratic institutions such as free media, free public debate and the right to speak openly, the democratic framework of 'checks and balances' of its own leaders limits the ability of an administration, a group or a government to launch wars or to use military force independently without essential public responsibility like for example in autocratic states.

This opens the door for peaceful settlements of disputes among competing states and lowers the risk of surprise attacks.

And third, the aspect of electoral liability of a government of a liberal democracy lowers the risk of war substantially. Democratic elites have to focus their policies towards the next elections for being re-elected and for retaining their positions.[15]

The use of military force, a potentially bloody and costly activity, could easily become a 'boomerang' for an administration due to the fact that the population might perceive it as a failure or as unjust. For avoiding such electoral ouster, liberal democracies rather tend to negotiate instead of using military force.

"Illiberal statesman find that war with a liberal democracy would be extremely unpopular. Moreover, they begin to fear electoral ouster if they go to war against a fellow liberal democracy."[16]

---

[14] For an in-depth analysis, see e.g John M. Owen, 'How Liberalism Produces Democratic Peace', *International Security*, 19:2 (Fall 1994), pp. 87–125. Specifically, he points out that the prevention of war among liberal states through democratic institutions only work in combination with liberal 'ideology': "Liberal ideas form the independent variable. These ideas produce the ideology which prohibits war with fellow liberal democracies and sometimes and sometimes calls for war with illiberal states. The ideas also give rise to democratic institutions. *Working in tandem, the ideology and institutions push liberal democracies towards democratic peace*", at p. 101 (emphasis added).

[15] For an excellent overview concerning the institutional arguments, see Bruce Bueno de Mesquita/James D. Morrow/Randolph M. Siverson/Alastair Smith, 'An Institutional Explanation of the Democratic Peace', *American Political Science Review*, 93:4 (December 1999), pp. 791–807.

[16] John M. Owen, 'How Liberalism Produces Democratic Peace', *supra* note 15, at p. 101.

These three arguments within the rationalist explanation – namely the democratic system of legal and constitutional restraints, the domestic institutions within democracies as well as the dimension of the electoral aspect – form the institutional mechanism which explains the absence of war among democracies: the existence of democratic institutions which are based on the three above described features.

The constructivist explanation/The normative approach

The second, also very popular approach of explaining the absence of war among democracies is highly inspired by constructivist thinking. The two basic tenets of the constructivist school in international relations (IR) are "[first] that the structures of human association are determined primarily by shared ideas rather than material forces, and [second] that the identities and interests of purposive actors are constructed by these shared ideas rather than given by nature."[17] According to and following these normative arguments, the constructivist explanation of democratic peace is based on (man made) norms and values.

Due to the fact that liberal democracies share the same norms and values and therefore trust each other to a bigger extent, war among them is less likely to appear. This is the central mechanism of democratic peace within the constructivist explanation.

"Liberal democracies are believed reasonable, predictable, and trustworthy, because, because they are governed by their citizens' true interests, which harmonize with all individuals' true interests atound the world."[18]

Following this logic, liberal democracies will always be reluctant to use military force against their fellow democracies due to the fact that they will assume generally pacific intentions within the policies of their peers through shared values and norms such as human rights.

---

[17] Alexander Wendt, 'Social Theory of International Politics', Cambridge: Cambridge University Press, 1999, p.1.
[18] John M. Owen, 'How Liberalism Produces Democratic Peace', *supra* note 15, at p. 95.

As Bruce Russett formulates it, this community of values of liberal democracies creates an atmosphere of "live and let live" among them and leads to the absence of war between these states.[19]

The interdependance approach

The interdependance approach for explaining democratic peace, only a minor form of explanation of liberal peace, sees reasons of economic interconnection between liberal democracies at the foreground. The free-market economies of democratic states are highly incentive for trade among each other which in turn increases the interdependance as well as the transnational ties among the trading partners. The economic dependance on trade within most sophisticated economies today include a strong interest in further deepening and lower the risk of a military conflict between partners due to the inherent negative impacts for their economy.[20]

This approach has been discussed highly controversial due to the fact that its arguments are very vulnerable. For example, the economic interdependence between European great powers right before World War I was comparably high but did not hinder the outbreak of war.

Democratic peace and democracies at war

Although a dissenting minority critizises for example the statistical relevance of democratic peace theory[21], points out that liberal democracies are historically too young for a valid proposition or that the hard cases for proving the theory are flawed[22], the absence of war among liberal democracies is obviously empirically provable.

---

[19] See, inter alia, Zeev Maoz/Bruce M. Russett, "Normative and Structural Causes of Democratic Peace, 1946–1986," *supra* note 13. For a critical discussion on (inter alia) that issue, see Bruce Russett/Christopher Layne/David E. Spiro/Michael W. Doyle,'Correspondence – The Democratic Peace', *International Security* 19:4 (Spring 1995), pp. 164-184.

[20] See e.g. John R. Oneal and Bruce M. Russett, 'The Classical Liberals Were Right: Democracy, Interdependence, and Conflict, 1950–1985', *International Studies Quarterly*, 41:2 (June 1997), pp. 267–294.

[21] See David E. Spiro, 'The Insignificance of the Liberal Peace', *supra* note 5.

[22] See Christopher Layne, 'Kant or Cant: The Myth of the Democratic Peace', *supra* note 5.

The criticism toward that theory remains, in Michael W. Doyle's words, on a "nitpicking" level e.g. of discussing 'near misses' of war, of moaning about how to cut and interpret statistical data or of disputing about if Finland was truly at war with other democracies during World War II or not.[23]

But, although liberal states are more peaceful among each other, with recent developments and conflicts á la Kosovo, Afghanistan and Iraq it becomes obviously clear that democratic peace does not necessarily mean peaceful democracies.

Liberal democracies are increasingly engaged in wars with non-democracies and are, in this regard, NOT reluctant to use military force. The question is if this situation is also explainable with the explanations for democratic peace and their inherent mechanisms described above. Therefore, I will compare the mechanisms of the two major ways of explaining democratic peace, namely the rationalist and the constructivist approach, with democracies using military force.

First, I want to analyze how the constructivist explanation which builds on a democratic peace mechanism of shared norms and values would see democracies using military force. While believing liberal democracies are somehow a community of values with trust and pacifism as main pillars, a democracy using military force against another democracy would be seen as almost unacceptable.

But, while liberal democracies "are believed reasonable, predictable, and trustworthy"[24], the contrary situation is the case with non-democracies. In this way of normative thinking, non-democracies are *a priori* illegitimate, untrustworthy and potentially hostile. Therefore the use of military force against them can become easily 'legitimate' and would not dissent the causal logic of democratic peace.

Only members of the community of values should not be attacked and the major goal should be that the whole world is part of that community. Having in mind that Western

---

[23] See Bruce Russett/Christopher Layne/David E. Spiro/Michael W. Doyle,'Correspondence – The Democratic Peace', *supra* note 20.
[24] See *supra* note 19.

liberal states developed concepts like for example *regime change*, this seems to be real in practise.

Second, I want to have a deeper look on the institutionalist/rationalist explanation of democratic peace and how it goes conform with democracies using military force. According to this approach, the causal mechanism of democratic institutions hinders the wage of war among democracies.

It would be hard to get public support for a war against a fellow liberal state, and even if one gets the support on the short-term, electoral punishment would be probable. But democratic institutions doe not make war impossible. While "using the same institutions of free discussion and the threat of electoral punishment, liberals may force their leaders into war."[25]

But, while fearing the consequences of failure in a system of democratic institutions, the leaders have to try harder to win wars and they try to get only engaged in conflicts they think to may win. While knowing that this will be same on the other side with a democratic enemy – namely that both sides trying hard and mobilizing every resource which might make a conflict long and bloody due to the fact that both sides fear electoral punishment – democratic enemies prefer rather to negotiate than to fight a war.

---

[25] John M. Owen, 'How Liberalism Produces Democratic Peace', *supra* note 15, at p. 101.